BUILDING BIG
CLASSICAL
ARCHITECTURE

by Joyce Markovics

CHERRY LAKE PRESS
cherrylakepublishing.com

Published in the United States of America by Cherry Lake Publishing Group
Ann Arbor, Michigan
www.cherrylakepublishing.com

Reading Adviser: Beth Walker Gambro, MS, Ed., Reading Consultant, Yorkville, IL
Content Adviser: Jeffrey Shumaker, AICP, Urban Designer, Planner, Architect, and Educator
Book Designer: Ed Morgan

Photo Credits: unsplash.com/Simone Hutsche, cover; unsplash.com/Marcus Spiske, title page; unsplash.com/Gabriella Clare Marino, 4–5; unsplash.com/Evan Qu, 6; Wikimedia Commons/Jean-Pierre Lavoie, 7; © Aerial-motion/Shutterstock, 8–9; freepik.com, 10; Public Domain, 11; unsplash.com/micheile dot com, 12–13; unsplash.com/Spencer Davis, 14–15; Wikimedia Commons/Carole Raddato, 15; Wikimedia Commons, 16; Wikimedia Commons, 17; freepik.com, 18–19; freepik.com, 21 top; freepik.com, 21 bottom; freepik.com, 22–23; © Ana Rodriguez Moreno/Shutterstock, 23 top; flickr/vince42, 24; unsplash.com/LoboStudio Hamburg, 25; flickr/vJohn Brighenti, 26–27.

Cherry Lake Press is an imprint of Cherry Lake Publishing Group.

Library of Congress Cataloging-in-Publication Data

Names: Markovics, Joyce L., author.
Title: Classical architecture / by Joyce Markovics.
Description: Ann Arbor, Michigan : Cherry Lake Publishing, [2023] | Series: Building big : amazing architecture | Includes bibliographical references and index. | Audience: Grades 4-6
Identifiers: LCCN 2022039586 (print) | LCCN 2022039587 (ebook) | ISBN 9781668919828 (hardcover) | ISBN 9781668924839 (paperback) | ISBN 9781668923504 (adobe pdf) | ISBN 9781668922170 (ebook) | ISBN 9781668924839 (kindle edition) | ISBN 9781668926161 (epub)
Subjects: LCSH: Architecture, Classical–Juvenile literature. | Classicism in architecture–Juvenile literature.
Classification: LCC NA260 .M395 2023 (print) | LCC NA260 (ebook) | DDC 722/.8–dc23/eng/20220824
LC record available at https://lccn.loc.gov/2022039586
LC ebook record available at https://lccn.loc.gov/2022039587

Printed in the United States of America
Corporate Graphics

CONTENTS

The Pantheon .4

What Is Classical Architecture? . . .10

Greek Architecture 12

Roman Architecture 16

The Renaissance and Beyond 20

Neoclassical Buildings 26

Design a Classical Building 28

Glossary 30

Read More 31

Learn More Online 31

Index 32

About the Author 32

The Pantheon

Tucked away in the streets of Rome, Italy, is an amazing building that's more than 2,000 years old! Called the Pantheon (PAN-thee-on), it's one of the best-preserved buildings of ancient Rome. It's also an excellent example of classical architecture. Made from concrete and brick, the round building has an enormous dome. Huge columns along the Pantheon's front side, or portico, support the roof. Above the columns is a section called a **pediment**. Here there's an **inscription**. It says that Marcus Agrippa built this. Agrippa was an architect and leader. And he was a close friend of Augustus, the first Roman emperor. Agrippa likely designed the original Pantheon to remember an important battle. However, it's thought that between 114 and 128 CE, other Roman emperors and their architects redesigned the Pantheon. These emperors include Trajan and Hadrian.

The Pantheon in Rome, Italy, dates to 27 BCE. The word *Pantheon* comes from a Greek word meaning "temple of the gods."

FACT BOX

An architect is a person who designs buildings. Architecture is the art of designing buildings.

The Pantheon's dome and oculus

When visitors step through the 24-foot- (7-meter-) tall heavy bronze doors of the Pantheon, they are often left speechless. The giant dome soars 71 feet (22 m) high and stretches 142 feet (43 m) across. When it was built, it was the largest dome of its kind. Architect and historian Mark Wilson Jones remembers how he felt the first time he entered the **monument**. "You are uplifted. You feel a kind of joy being in the presence of such an extraordinary thing," Jones said.

At the center of the top of the dome is a 27-foot (8-m) round window called an oculus—the Latin word for "eye." The oculus allows sunlight to flood the Pantheon's interior space. This was a groundbreaking achievement at the time. In the past, architects focused their attention on the exteriors of buildings. The Pantheon is different. Its exterior is plain. However, its interior is covered with colorful marble, detailed carvings, and sunken square panels called coffers. The coffers are divided into 28 sections, which equal the number of columns inside the building.

Some of the columns and colorful marble in the Pantheon's interior

FACT BOX

A floor plan is a diagram that shows the arrangement of rooms in a building.

Experts are still unsure how exactly the Pantheon's dome was built. They do know ancient builders used bricks, **mortar**, and concrete. Concrete is a building material developed by the Romans using a mixture of sand, rocks, and water. Before it dries and hardens, concrete can be made into different shapes. The Romans used it to build **aqueducts**, bridges, and domes. Experts like Mark Wilson Jones also know the Pantheon has 20-foot- (6-m-) thick walls that help support its gigantic dome. They believe the top part of the dome was built using lightweight concrete to keep it from collapsing. To make this special concrete, the Romans used pumice (PUHM-is). This type of stone is light enough to float in water. Still, questions remain. As experts learn more about the Pantheon, they agree it's one of the most important classical buildings ever built. To this day, it inspires architecture all over the world.

Here is the Pantheon's gigantic dome
and oculus as seen from above.

What Is Classical Architecture?

All buildings—old and new—are created using architecture, a combination of science and art. Architects use different elements to express their vision for a building. For example, they consider shape, size, building materials, and other factors. However, architects are not like sculptors who create artworks purely for their own sake. Architecture has a purpose, which is to create a physical place for people. One of an architect's main jobs is to figure out how a building will be used and who will use it.

The U.S. Capitol building is a modern-day example of classical architecture.

Throughout history, there have been various styles of architecture. Classical architecture is one of the most **iconic** and widespread. The main feature of this style is symmetry (SIM-ih-tree). Symmetry is an equal distribution of parts. For example, sections that mirror each other, like the two halves of an apple, are symmetrical. Symmetry gives architecture balance and order. Proportion is another key element of classical architecture. It's the relationship between different parts and how they look as a whole.

This painting by the Italian artist Pietro Perugino from 1481 to 1482 shows symmetry. The two halves of the painting mirror each other.

Certain building materials also characterize classical architecture. These include stone such as marble, brick, and concrete.

Greek Architecture

Classical architecture started with the Greeks and Romans. Ancient Greece was a **civilization** in southeastern Europe. It existed more than 2,000 years ago and was made up of hundreds of cities known as city-states. Ancient Greece was a place where art, science, **philosophy**, and architecture thrived. "Nothing to excess" was the Greeks' guiding rule. The ancient Greeks celebrated beauty and balance. And they contributed one of the most important elements to classical architecture.

Ancient Greek ruins showing Corinthian columns and capitals

Though they did not invent the column, the Greeks created three main styles, or orders, of columns. These are Doric, Ionic, and Corinthian. Each column type has a unique design, known as a capital, on the top. Doric capitals have little decoration. Ionic capitals have a scroll-like decoration on either side of the capital. Corinthian capitals are the most **ornate** and include carved **acanthus** leaves that curve up and out from the capital.

The three main types of Greek columns: Doric, Corinthian, and Ionic

FACT BOX

Caryatids (kar-ee-AT-i-deedz) are Greek columns in the shape of female figures.

The ancient Greeks built marble or stone buildings using columns and other features. Most Greek temples, for example, had a porch called a portico and a rectangular foundation. One of the most celebrated examples of ancient Greek architecture—called the Parthenon—sits on a hill in Athens, Greece. Dating to 438 BCE, it's an almost perfectly symmetrical marble temple with Doric columns. To form the columns, ancient builders stacked carved pieces of stone. Above the columns were once sculpted panels called friezes (FREEZ-ez) that showed battle scenes.

The Parthenon in Athens, Greece

The ancient Greek Theatre of Epidaurus

Another defining example of Greek architecture is the Theatre of Epidaurus. The outdoor theater measures 387 feet (118 m) in diameter and could seat as many as 13,000 people! From its raised **tiers**, ancient Greeks sat and watched plays. Made from limestone, it's the first all-stone theater the Greeks built. And it remains one of the most outstanding outdoor theaters ever built.

FACT BOX

Some of the seats in the Theatre of Epidaurus have carvings on them with the names of ancient **donors**!

Roman Architecture

After the Greeks came the Romans. Their civilization was centered around the city of Rome. By the year 200, Rome likely had a population of more than 1 million people! The Romans spread out across Europe, Asia, Africa, and other parts of the world. They were heavily influenced by the Greeks but made their own contributions to **engineering** and architecture. In fact, the Romans not only developed aqueducts and concrete, they also created bathhouses, plumbing, and roads and highways. In addition, they added the Composite order to the three types of columns. It's a combination of the Ionic and Corinthian columns.

Pont du Gard is an ancient Roman aqueduct bridge in France.

Marcus Vitruvius was an important Roman architect and engineer. He wrote a multi-volume book around 15 BCE about architecture that focused on three principles—strength, functionality, and beauty. According to Vitruvius, a building's designs should relate to the symmetry of the human body. He believed this would create *eurythmia*, the Latin word for "good proportion."

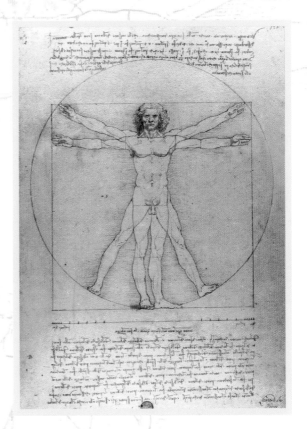

Leonardo da Vinci's *The Vitruvian Man*

FACT BOX

Leonardo da Vinci came up with a drawing based on Vitruvius's ideas about the symmetry of the human body. He called it *The Vitruvian Man* and said, "Man is the model of the world." Like Vitruvius, Da Vinci believed in a strong connection between the human form and architecture.

This is an image of the Colosseum, which dates from 80 CE. The entrance was called the *vomitorium*. Why? That's where people would "spill in" like the forceful flow of vomit.

Roman architecture was less plain that Greek architecture. It also introduced a new element—the arch. Arches made it possible to span greater distances and support more weight. The Romans used arches in much of their architecture, such as in bridges, aqueducts, and arenas. Roman emperors also built giant arches to signify their **conquests**. Some arches, like Constantine's in Rome, Italy, used sculptures to tell stories of war. One of the most famous ancient Roman structures is the Colosseum (kol-uh-SEE-uhm). This giant **amphitheater**, also located in Rome, has seating for 50,000 people!

The Arch of Constantine, which is next to the Colosseum, was built in the year 312.

The seating is arranged around a central oval-shaped open space where staged battles between **gladiators** and wild animals would take place. The Romans built the huge Colosseum using arches and columns made from stone and concrete. The amphitheater even had a massive **retractable** awning that shielded people from the Sun. The Romans built many other magnificent structures until their empire fell in the year 476.

The Romans used enslaved people to build the Colosseum over 10 years. Experts believe as many as 500,000 people and 1 million animals were killed during the battles held there.

The Renaissance and Beyond

After the Roman empire, classical architecture spread across Europe. Over time, it included new elements. For example, during the Romanesque (roh-muh-NESK) period in the years 1000 to 1150, taller, rounder arches appeared. In addition, **steeples** were introduced. They commonly appeared on churches. Following Romanesque architecture came Gothic. This style focused on light and height! Gothic architecture included stained-glass windows to let in as much light as possible. To raise ceiling heights, architects developed pointed arches and stone vaults. A vault is a self-supported arched form that covers a large space. Gothic architecture also used the flying buttress. A flying buttress is an external support that helped hold up a tall building, such as a church. The most notable Gothic architecture can be seen in large churches called cathedrals. The best examples are in Europe.

An example of Gothic architecture is the Notre Dame Cathedral in Paris, France. The flying buttresses can be seen on the outside of the building.

FACT BOX

Gothic architecture showcased lots of sculpture. Gargoyles (GAHR-goilz) are scary-looking carved human or animal faces that carry rainwater away from a building. They were also believed to protect a church from bad spirits!

The Italian Renaissance (run-uh-SAHNS) followed the Gothic period. It was at its height between 1400 and 1600 in Italy. The word *renaissance* means "rebirth." This was a time when art and science thrived. Also, the work of ancient Greeks and Romans was rediscovered. Filippo Brunelleschi (1377–1446) was a great Renaissance architect. Born in Florence, Italy, he was hired by the Medicis, a wealthy and powerful family, to build a cathedral. He built the *Duomo* (DWOH-moh), the Italian word for "dome." Brunelleschi figured out how to build it by putting one dome inside another. So, the inner dome supported the outer one.

FACT BOX

An inscription on Filippo Brunelleschi's tomb reads, "A man of great genius." Brunelleschi was also a fine artist.

The Duomo in Florence, Italy

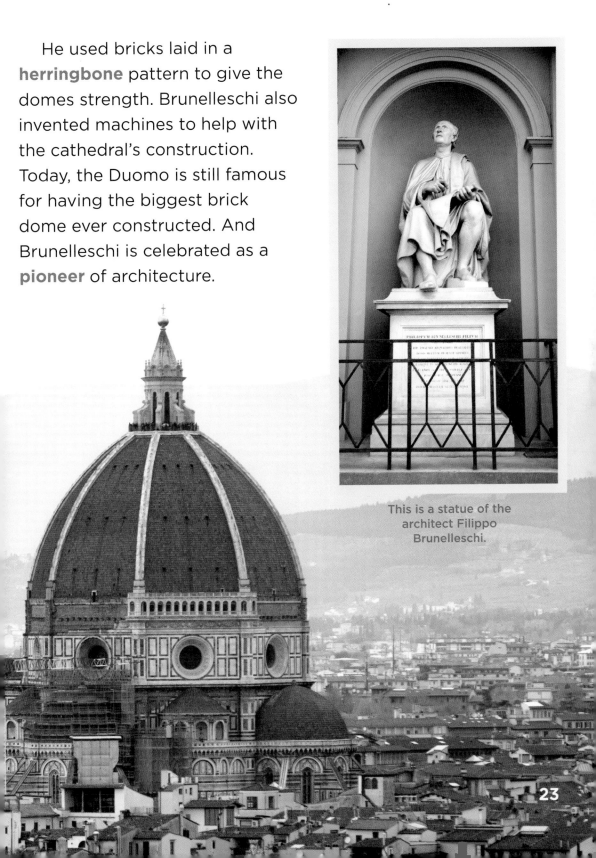

He used bricks laid in a **herringbone** pattern to give the domes strength. Brunelleschi also invented machines to help with the cathedral's construction. Today, the Duomo is still famous for having the biggest brick dome ever constructed. And Brunelleschi is celebrated as a **pioneer** of architecture.

This is a statue of the architect Filippo Brunelleschi.

Andrea Palladio (1508–1580) also based his work on Greek and Roman architecture. He was one of the most influential architects of the Renaissance. Palladio studied the work of ancient buildings and architects. During his lifetime, he designed 30 large country homes, or villas. His most well-known villa is La Rotonda. It's a beautifully symmetrical home on a hill. "The loveliest hills are arranged around it," wrote Palladio. He also wrote a famous essay that became a cornerstone of modern architecture.

Andrea Palladio designed Villa La Rotonda in 1566.

Sanssouci Palace in Germany

The Baroque (buh-ROHK) period came next and lasted from around 1600 to 1830. This style combined classical elements with lots of **embellishments**. Baroque buildings were highly detailed and grand. For example, architects used many curved shapes, gold, and carvings, including chubby angels, called cherubs, in their designs. The style became widespread. The best-known Baroque buildings include the Palace of Versailles in France and the Sanssouci Palace in Germany.

FACT BOX

Andrea Palladio's work was so important that an architectural style was named after him. It's called Palladian architecture.

Neoclassical Buildings

After a while, people grew tired of all of the elaborate details of Baroque architecture. As a reaction to it, architects once again turned to classical architecture—with some updates. This period (1730–1925) was known as Neoclassicism (nee-oh-KLAS-uh-siz-uhm). Architects who worked during this time combined classical features with modern touches.

In the United States, neoclassical architecture became very popular. Many government buildings in Washington, DC, were built in this stately style. This was a way of linking the young nation with the ideals of ancient Greece and Rome. Neoclassicism spread across the country. Architects used the style in courthouses, banks, schools, churches, and homes throughout the United States. Many of these buildings are still standing. And classical elements, such as columns, still appear in new architecture today!

FACT BOX

Pompeii was a Roman city that was buried by an **eruption** of Mount Vesuvius in 79 BCE. The ruins were discovered in 1709. This brought about a renewed interest in classical Greek and Roman architecture.

Design a Classical Building

Think about what you just learned about classical architecture in this book. Now use that information to design your own classical or neoclassical building!

DESIGN CONCEPT: What is your idea for your building? Where will it be located? What will it be used for? What materials will you use to build it? Consider your building's form *and* function.

PLAN: Think about what the exterior and interior of your building will look like. How will it incorporate classical features, such as columns, a portico, pediment, or dome? How big or small will it be?

DRAW: Grab some paper and a pencil. Sketch the floor plan of your building to show the arrangement of rooms. Label each room. Next, draw the exterior, noting what materials will be used.

BUILD A MODEL: Use materials around your home, such as clay, paper, cardboard, scissors, straws, popsicle sticks, and glue, to build a small model of your building.

REFINE YOUR PLAN: What works about your design? What doesn't work? Make any needed changes to improve your building.

GLOSSARY

acanthus (uh-KAN-thus) resembling the leaves of a plant that has spiny leaves

amphitheater (AM-fuh-thee-uh-ter) an open-air stadium in ancient Rome

aqueducts (AK-wih-duhkts) channels for holding and carrying water

civilization (siv-uh-luh-ZEY-shuhn) the society, culture, and way of life of a particular area

conquests (KON-kwests) battles to take control of something

donors (DOH-nurz) people who contribute to something

embellishments (em-BEL-ish-muhnts) decorations

engineering (en-jun-NIHR-ing) the science of building things

eruption (i-RUP-shun) the sending out of lava, ash, steam, and gas from a volcano

gladiators (GLAD-ee-ey-terz) ancient Roman fighters

herringbone (HER-ing-bohn) a pattern made up of vertical rows of slanting lines that form Vs

iconic (ahy-KIN-ik) respected

inscription (in-SKRP-shuhn) words marked into something

monument (MON-yuh-muhnt) a building or other structure built to honor a famous person or event

mortar (MOR-tur) a mixture of sand, lime, water, and cement that is spread and hardened between bricks or stones to hold them together

ornate (AWR-neyt) elaborately decorated

pediment (PED-uh-muhnt) the triangular upper part of the front of a building

philosophy (fuh-LOSS-uh-fee) the study of the nature of things

pioneer (pye-uh-NEER) the first person to do something

retractable (ri-TRAKT-uh-buhl) able to be moved back and forth

steeples (STEE-puhlz) tall towers

tiers (TEERZ) one of a series of rows of seats

READ MORE

Allen, Peter. *Atlas of Amazing Architecture*. London: Cicada Books, 2021.

Armstrong, Simon. *Cool Architecture*. London: Pavilion, 2015.

Dillon, Patrick. *The Story of Buildings*. Somerville, MA: Candlewick Press, 2014.

Glancey, Jonathan. *Architecture: A Visual History*. London: DK, 2021.

Moreno, Mark. *Architecture for Kids*. Emeryville, VA: Rockridge Press, 2021.

LEARN MORE ONLINE

Architecture for Children
https://archforkids.com

Britannica Kids: Architecture
https://kids.britannica.com/students/article/architecture/272939

Center for Architecture: Architecture at Home Resources
https://www.centerforarchitecture.org/k-12/resources/

Lego Design Challenge
https://www.architects.org/uploads/BSA_LWW_LEGO_Challenge.pdf

STEAM Exercises: Kid Architecture
http://www.vancebm.com/kidArchitect/pages/steamExercises.html

INDEX

Agrippa, Marcus, 4
aqueducts, 8, 16, 18
arches, 18–20
architects, 4–7, 10, 17, 20, 22, 24–27
Arch of Constantine, 18–19
Baroque period, 25
brick, 11, 22–23
Brunelleschi, Filippo, 22–23
caryatids, 13
cathedrals, 20–23
classical architecture
   defining, 10
   design your own, 28–29
   elements of, 11
coffers, 7
Colosseum, 18–19
columns, 4, 7, 12–14, 16, 19, 27
Composite order, 16
concrete, 4, 8, 11, 16, 19
Corinthian columns, 13
da Vinci, Leonardo, 17
domes, 4, 6–8
Doric columns, 13
Duomo, the, 22–23
enslaved workers, 19
floor plan, 7
flying buttresses, 20
gargoyles, 21
Gothic period, 20

Greek architecture, 12–15
Ionic columns, 13
Italian Renaissance, 22–24
Jones, Mark Wilson, 6, 8
marble, 7, 11, 14
Neoclassicism, 26–27
Notre Dame Cathedral, 21
oculus, 6–7, 9
Palace of Versailles, 25
Palladian architecture, 25
Palladio, Andrea, 24–25
Pantheon, 4–9
Parthenon, 14
Pompeii, 27
Pont du Gard, 16
porticos, 4, 14, 29
Renaissance architecture, 20–24
Roman architecture, 4–9, 16–19
Roman engineering, 16
Romanesque period, 20
Sanssouci Palace, 25
steeples, 20
symmetry, 10–11, 14, 17
Theatre of Epidaurus, 15
U.S. Capitol building, 10
Villa La Rotonda, 24
Vitruvius, Marcus, 17
Washington, DC, 27

ABOUT THE AUTHOR

Joyce Markovics has written hundreds of books for young readers. She lives in a nearly 200-year-old carpenter Gothic style house along the Hudson River. Joyce would like to thank architect, designer, and city planner Jeff Shumaker for his insight and help creating this series. She dedicates this book